# Books by Michael Daley

## POETRY
### CHAPBOOKS
*Angels*
*Yes: Five Poems*
*The Corn Maiden*
*Original Sin*
*Rosehip Plum Cherry*
*Awakening in 5 Irish Towns*

### COLLECTIONS
*The Straits*
*To Curve*
*Moonlight in the Redemptive Forest*
*Of a Feather*
*True Heresies*
*Born With*

## ESSAYS
*Way Out There*

## ANTHOLOGIES
*In Our Hearts & Minds: The Pacific Northwest & Central America,*
*The Dalmo'ma Anthology*

## TRANSLATIONS
*Alter Mundus by Lucia Gazzino*
*Horace: Eleven Odes*

# Born With

*Michael Daley*

MICHAEL
DALEY

*for Bill Porter*
*good friend & true supporter*
*of this art we somehow*
*get away with*

*June 6, 2020*

DOS MADRES

2020

## DOS MADRES PRESS INC.
P.O. Box 294, Loveland, Ohio 45140
www.dosmadres.com    editor@dosmadres.com

Dos Madres is dedicated to the belief that the small press is essential to the vitality of contemporary literature as a carrier of the new voice, as well as the older, sometimes forgotten voices of the past. And in an ever more virtual world, to the creation of fine books pleasing to the eye and hand.

Dos Madres is named in honor of Vera Murphy and Libbie Hughes, the "Dos Madres" whose contributions have made this press possible.

Dos Madres Press, Inc. is an Ohio Not For Profit Corporation and a 501 (c) (3) qualified public charity. Contributions are tax deductible.

Executive Editor: Robert J. Murphy

Illustration & Book Design: Elizabeth H. Murphy
www.illusionstudios.net

Cover Photo By Ansel Adams - U.S. National Archives and Records Administration, Public Domain, https://commons.wikimedia.org/w/index.php?curid=17174349

Typeset in Adobe Garamond Pro
ISBN 978-1-948017-85-5
Library of Congress Control Number: 2020936695

# ACKNOWLEDGEMENTS

Versions of these poems first appeared thanks to the editors of:
*At the Water's Edge* (Cow Field Mist Dusk)
*Bijou Poetry Review* (Spade)
*Bozalta Collective* (To the Father of the Drowned Refugee Child)
*Burningword Literary Journal* (Poem Interrupted by AM Radio
    New York City 1984)
*Cascadia Review* (Two Rivers)
*Cirque* (Among School Children; Ars Poetica)
*Cleaver* (After the Tremors)
*Clover* (Field Stones; Snow on the Chuckanuts; Insomnia,
    Quiet House; Late Twentieth Century)
*Conversations across Borders* (Furnace)
*Empty Bowl Broadsides* (Song 49; Water Street & Taylor)
*Fault Lines* (A Prayer for the Republic in Despair)
*Floating Bridge Review* (Furnace; To Love)
*Fungi Magazine* (The Virgin Knife)
*Gargoyle* (Grace)
*Ghost Town Poetry Anthology* (The Death of a Sparrow Hawk)
*Minotaur* (Shaggy Mane)
*North American Review* (Song 49)
*Pictures of Poets* (Field Stones)
*Raven Chronicles* (Shaggy Mane; The Virgin Knife; One For the
    Road)
*Rhino* (Cow Field Mist Dusk)
*Sage Green Journal* (To Love)
*Shantii Journal* (Children of the Storm)
*Tangram* (The Last Master)
*Terrain.org* (Denied a Certain Reach for Joy)
*WA 129 Anthology* (In Memory)
*Wallpaper* (To the Father of the Drowned Refugee Child)
*Empty Bowl* published the chapbook, *Awakening in 5 Irish Towns*.

A deep bow of respect and gratitude to Robert and Elizabeth Murphy of Dos Madres for their integrity and the care they've given these poems. I'm very grateful to friends who made valuable editorial suggestions while this manuscript evolved: Tim McNulty, Mike O'Connor, Holly Hughes, Finn Wilcox, and Bill Porter. I'm especially grateful to the universe for Kathy Prunty, and grateful to her for her sharp eye and her brave love.

for Theo

# TABLE OF CONTENTS

## 1.

## 2.

## 3.

# 4.

On one occasion, we posted the hunter in such a way that the fox ran straight at Vladimir Ilyich. He seized his gun, but the fox, after standing and looking at him a moment, darted away into the wood. We were puzzled: 'Why on earth didn't you shoot?' We asked. 'Well—he was so beautiful, you know,' said Vladimir Ilyich.

—*Nadezhda Krupskaya*


Before us the thick dark current runs. It talks up to us in a murmur become ceaseless and myriad, the yellow surface dimpled monstrously into fading swirls travelling along the surface for an instant, silent, impermanent and profoundly significant, as though just beneath the surface something huge and alive waked for a moment of lazy alertness out of and into light slumber again.

—*William Faulkner*

1.

# AMONG SCHOOL CHILDREN

In a photograph by Alice Austen,
*Suspender Salesman Wall Street 1896,*
two emotions crest over the subject's face—
distrust of fashion's caprice
and confidence in man's need to hold up his pants.

In the harbor behind him squeals carom off
the brick walls of America's accounting industry.
At each desk a pair of suspenders
wriggles across the muscles of scribes.

In 1953, style gave way to stiletto belts,
but my mother cinched me into suspenders,
pushed me to the street, off to First Grade.

I finger-painted my white shirt in Miss Nealy's classroom,
but, thumbs stained on the oozing inkwell,
I squirmed out of my last seat in the last row,
the iron desk dripping gibberish,
and jolted over the desktops.

What else could she or any young woman have done?
We clutched with our tiniest fingertips pen nibs
to scrawl our names on damp paper. For her.

I've lifted hundreds out of sorrow with my story.
If I've known you a week, I've told it three times.
My classmates squealed as I soared around the room.
Miss Nealy lunged at my blond eggshell skull,

squeezed my rubbery shoulders and lashed me
to the cold seat with my dapper red suspenders.

In resounding silence, everyone upright, bright and tall,
those faces I loved turn to my criminal's corner
and into our dim capacity for irony
the fire bell bleats off old brick walls.

After a lifetime, I understand her calm, her need
to reassure us—we were babies—but I knew then—
her eyes on me—my best friends giggling as they filed
to safety, some looking back—her eyes on me,
that silent glare from my first cherished Muse—
I knew she would leave me to burn.

*for Johnny McDonough*

## FURNACE

We are in the cellar shoveling coal.
She shovels. I'm five. She's angry.
Not with me—Christ, I brighten the cave.
In cowboy pajamas I shine
the ceiling with quivering flashlight.

My memory freezes her bent to the shovel
in cocktail waitress skirt and white blouse,
in nylons and heels. She clanks the coal-chute,
flames roar out the iron door, God's claw.

Out of love, my father, his fingers caging a shot glass,
calculates her work for tips from drunks with sideburns.
Black moles of his eyes dissolve my childhood.
He descends like ash
down a burning well a hundred meters wide.
What a diamond is his mind.

We live on Annabel Street
where we play Freeze Tag.
They said we could never die.
Coal kept us safe. Stop! I froze us.

The planet didn't ricochet.
No oil spill rings the moon.
Nothing changed. I'm *It*.

# FIELD STONES

### 1.

After I hug them up from dirt
the crush of eons rubs grit into my palms,
grinds down my fingerprint.
Like anonymous peasants, I lug piles from the lumpy field,
payoff behind the plow, to load the catapult.
Thatch roof yields like gossamer.
Go tell Uncle I split my head open.
He better gather up cobweb to heal.
Even with half a brain I can toss a rock.

My wheelbarrow drops three stones,
tribal dark where the lightening got out.
I tilt them onto the top of the firepit,
but the weightiest topples, splits in two,
surface clean as asteroid face down in black ash.

Tilth goes looking for buttercup
under cleft stone, flat slate, under blue oval.
In smeared and crumbled sandstone
worms uncork in blind chill summer.

### 2.

My father unearthed them too,
his knees in gravel and granite
setting a flagstone step to descend the porch
for feet as small as hers.

Near his hospital I loitered beside historic sunken slabs,
harsh records in quarry stone,
whole families scattered through soil below frost.
Not ours. We're lost somewhere on a distant mound.

### 3.

Up a ladder, healing a window with a knife,
he taught me resentment descends from its ape, approval.
I'm finally mourning today.
I had no time he might spend on me.
I ran over the broken glass in car lots
where a cracked-up fleet of Pontiacs sank to their rims.
The streetlight hummed over kids who walloped
melt tar out of summer potholes.

Maybe he wanted to teach me
when he said, *You don't know anything,*
but, stung for my life, I ran.
He never saw my wind-up and pitch,
the strike I chucked down Annabel
after a raid on the graveyard rockpile.
Provocative—stoned the way the martyrs were,
I was only hit twice by rocks lobbed like stricken ducks.

### 4.

I haul off stones till the Pleiades clambers up the East
and slump onto damp grass,
three field stones on my chest weigh down my ribcage,
backbone nudged, lungs flattening.
I promise my body, You won't die in exile
and my eyes close on rocks upon rocks.

He was the good man who took a lifetime to know,
or imagine I know.
Wheeling him into sunlight, he's in hospice robe.
We're trapped together after years.

He weeps almost casually,
so, we talk about the workmen in brittle sun
against that rocky soil just out the window,
and what a tough job they have,
digging the boulders out of the earth.

*for my sister, Maureen Louzan*

## A Poem Interrupted by AM Radio, New York City, 1984

When the radio blasted over the art gallery
and Jim Morrison crashed my only reading in the Big Apple,
eyes of famous poets in the audience
averted from my broken smile
and I flew away, I wasn't there—I went way past the headlights,
out past our unrecorded tribal rubric,
airwaves drumming through me
and huddled at a hideout on my own back streets.
Jimmy Wardell's yard, 1957, one sticky afternoon
when we beat each other up on the same wedge of dirt
my mother, a little girl, played hopscotch on in 1929
between Cronin's barn and a paint peel
on the fence of a three-decker—
who knows who lived there—Cid Corman maybe
who mooned down Annabel muttering blessings.

That afternoon, my smile might have made you grimace, too.
It does me as my fingerprints corrode this yellowed polaroid
the hostess was so quick to shoot
before unplugging *Riders on the Storm*.
My father's gift for the rare true smile
and my grandmother—cloud hair, morbidly soft skin,
and tyrannical—
come back alive again, come back to me
through this photograph of a shudder
and a trace of alleys and shame in my disrupted line,
her only recorded history when, circa nineteen-ten,
she took the hand of the one who rolled our lopsided smile
down the staircase of the spine.

## To Love

When the priests in their beads and capes
stitched from feral hides
led me under the New England pines,
they whittled the tip of a sawn limb
to gently press up through ribs
and the ventricular hollow
and on that spit their meaty hands
dipped me in the river
and as promised
I felt nothing
ever again
until you found me.

## Denied a Certain Reach for Joy

Hidden in a tree's annual deepening,
rings only begin to exist after the faller's saw,
in sweet fury, whines through a long afternoon.
The stones rattle an open secret in creek wash—
it's the end of wishes.
In my own vulnerable youth
so much was lost to a disguise—
how to say meant something more
than how to remember.
I know I thought I knew what it meant
to be hidden and monumental
and go unnoticed in the actual sunlight
yet I let nothing torture future me
who now pores over the pitch-sticky scent
off two hundred years of newly born rings on a stump
looking for a day when the truth cut me clean through.

# 2.

## WATER STREET & TAYLOR

An ode to dedication
*for he on honeydew hath fed*
*and drunk the milk of paradise*
Coleridge, *Kubla Kahn*


*After you left,* the Muse told me, the cold building
harbored artists and I remembered stairs squealing
when Bob hauled the letterpress beast up, then
years later set it down, regally, in a flatbed—
both ways on a taut come-along chain
cranked by three hearty guys promised beer—
*after you left,* she said, for years windows rattled
in the five unheated stories where
dancers, luthiers, weavers practiced—a masseuse,
a jeweler, poets, the madness of a cliff-dwelling painter,
his easel blood-spatter brittle in moon slash.
A golden age crackled in those street corner
rooms once-upon-a-time kerosene-lit for a hundred years
by whores and lonesome boys shipping out to Shanghai.
Artists paid rent with art, jugglers held open the doors,
and I, submissive citizen, sold the clock
tattooed to my body at infancy
far from that five-story throwback
across the sea from the sculptor's molten pour,
behind a boil of asymmetrical windows and tin,
a world away from a squat on the stone-cold floor
where French-garretted scribblers starved on crumbs
and tourist leftovers, drank in hymns
of humiliated monks on the mossy plaza
where the jeweler botched a Persian glaze on bone.
Heavy-helmeted artisans dripped silver
into sacramental alchemy and the ruins of Alexandria,

13

reawakened into this world, throbbed like furnace,
feathers of a toe dancer's slipper
lit by cold dawn flames.

# Awakening In 5 Irish Towns

*Appalled, I see the true shape of my hand*—Robert Sund

1.

*Cork*
This morning, like other mornings,
one hand tucked into the other,
I watch tap water fill the bowl they form,
but on its way to wash my eyes,
lifelines of the two palms foretell my heart's climate
and I spill cold water in a puddle at my foot,
the bowl of my fingers gone away
with all I knew was real while I dreamed.

*Galway*
A two-handed bowl, fingers curved,
thumbs joined inward, catches
a steady drip of rain, the ration of rice—
a figure of sorts for my generation's beggars.
I gave money to one who slept
in a strung-up net of plastic parts.
Beside the lit wind and fall of River Corrib
his brittle finger scalds the coin.

15

2.

*Cobh*
Among the three million émigrés
I wait centuries on the pier.
Viking bogs exhume my cliff-straggled arch.
Heel-bone sheathed, leggings didn't leak.
In the goodbye sop of a road,
cattle-bruised greens pitch forth the 13th century.
Where a crammed hedge hates the stone,
a jockey trots a chestnut mare in honey light.
Two boys of my families—O Fahy, Dalaigh—
sucked up rain from their hands
for frail nutrient and ate dirt, says Spencer,
who took a moment to peer out a window
before slaving again over *Fairy Queen.*

*

I didn't know I was a child.
The unchangeable went on unendingly.
*Hold them out,* ungloved fingers
took small bread, handful seeds.
She steps back, folds her arms.
Brave around the lips, the mother
and tears—wouldn't there have been tears?
And a joke: Ancient Aunt Hannah's Pajamas.
Before her palm formally lifts for *Stop*
or *Peace—the rest of your life,*
I ran off to huddle aboard steerage.

A blundered surge of sorrow decays into shrubs
stricken by a real (or else false) exploded heart.
A trumpet carouses the village roadside
as crowds of hand-weavers crack shells,
the sea-leg harvest—this now is the cutting edge.

\*

*Was that your hand?* Margaret Atwood asked,
who I thought might rob me of it for her novel.
At the party she meant, my right hand—shot out
(the rest of me thoughtless, uninformed, never
spilling a drop) to soften the iron Newell post
where the toddler tilted
in knocked backward wood highchair
and I seized her unstitched dewdrop skull,
held her safe there, her parents' arms empty,
their drinks shattered, out of love.

3.

*Limerick*
Of all the bridges to scramble across
in blowing sheets of rain,
on this one I find Eamon O Dalaigh.
His rebel ancestor statue hovers the wide ripple
Shannon's deep bowl hushes to Belfast.
Later I awoke, my clothes still drenched,
in a train car next to a man and woman
who knew him as Ned Daly,
citizens who barely could recall the Maze hunger-
strikers wiped out of history as if a tornado
scoured prayer beads from their hands.

The woman by her eyes leaves no doubt
I shall eat the sandwich.
She wrapped it for him, in smeared cellophane,
her hands thin, nails unpolished.
"You could have picked a dryer year," he says.
Probably I snored—old timer, my Yank backpack—
or sneezed anyway, cupped hand to nostril
to spirit away too soon my pneuma,
good Greek breath flung at spiritual pneumonia.

*Claddagh*
Two hands clasp to scoop from air
as if a bowl the spigot water ice
and lift above a porcelain sink
to my face to awaken eyes
out of how I so longed for sleep
only to look on azure sailing away

into curtains of cumuli
after which this bowl too vanishes
hands fold for pockets
fingers braille the teeth of a key
a language exact utilitarian
two gnarled petals of ennui idle until
they awaken unutterable welcome
to serve to save all my beloveds
from gravity's clutch

## In Memory

Seamus Heaney appeared to me last night,
*flicker-lit*, here beside the cool Skagit
where chatter of the kingfisher's heard most
beside a highway hollow as the mist,
apparition from whom I learn to read
on this silt bank where I believe the dead.
He says at two "Quads" music streams two ways
then he's shushed by a hushed afterlife nurse.
On a map the river, a root-twined nerve,
gouged glacier slopes polished as poetry.
Once in a hall he tuned to such a glow
I heard him admire as 'vegetative'
that tendril-soaked turf of early Roethke
and woke from sleep too soon to see him go.

*for Anne McCracken*

## After Rachel Carson

In whorls and under pools
     Charybdis stirs the deep
          so much the tide hurls
abyssal faces, she says:
     their atrophied eyes
          in starved sockets, phosphoric membranes—
memory without substance—
     against the lighthouse beach rocks
          at Messina.

Gravity tugs seawater,
     dripping off the oar on my shoulder.
I rise from surf and trudge inland
     to winnow out stones
          for the sea's altar.

Gravid with the 'outermost stars,'
     she feels edges of the universe
tug a vaster yield of ocean under full glow
     like last night's when smoke cleared
          a newborn full moon
lifted in bare upcurved arms
     of hemlock silhouette.

Twice a month the moon, sun and earth
     surge against Uncle Danny's corroded seawall

and his hand-hewn steps,
his skiff lifted high at the wharf.

Salted away,
        as forgotten wines
                will taste of vinegar,
stacks of his celestial driftwood
        spark from the fireplace,
                scorch Andromeda and
Alpheratz,
        the Horse's Ass,
                into his Turkish carpet.

Sun, moon's silver thread, and earth
        *triangulate neap tides,*
                *a narrowing and shallowing*
    untroubled breath
                of a sea monster,
        as ancients, she wrote,
                sang of our solar and lunar
rhythms.

# ARS POETICA

1.

I sketch the light in the husk of a bee,
but gray bits of eraser cling to my carpenter's pencil.
When I draw, I learn a new language—
in fog, clumping in my oxcart uphill.
A little wind swings the feeder pendulum true.
A hummingbird jolts my eye
to conceive a straight line.
The good rain hammers the beat.
My hat brim stashes its echoes
up from a splashed boot and a mucky cuff.
A feathery twinge allows a hope my hip won't quit.
Where etched cliffs trickle and creeks overflow onto stones,
I stop to sketch, but snow melt pours over my grave
continuous as a twirl of the wrist.

**2.**

My pencil wrinkled the line of encouragement
across a dancer's forehead,
and her crowd shouldered me off the curb.
I drew a sky in sheets of tin pulled back,
wind battered the dogwood slippers
and the sidewalk ballerina smashed the devil's dishes.

I want to shade in the sough
that lifts the boughs at rush hour.
When we inch along the Narrows Bridge
whose sway girders our inland sea,
a raging windstorm topples the semi.
In the flutter of little wings just below my ribcage
I'm suspended midair
above my own mortgage, taxes, shopping lists.
Above my own breath—for one second,
but when I sketch the sparks behind wind
I'm back in the flow of traffic.

3.

I draw a clutter for clematis, for its white mercy shed—
white flame, white smoke, a wing too stubborn to quit.
Dawn's no miracle, but ordinary time throws
cloud-inked petals to wheel the stars.

This rain—brushed in streaks sideways.
A sudden wash of weeds on the pavement.
Rain with the smirk of a boy in my old schoolyard
flipping pebbles at his elegant sisters
who pelted him with snowballs
till he couldn't stand.
This rain is like that.
You can't escape.
Everything will be just fine,
beloved puppy.

4.

I leave a pebble in the corner,
drop a sprig of eucalyptus.
My ancestor bred of 'wicked stealthy guile'
sneaked a skiff out of the harbor
under half a crooked moon
not nearly as broken as this.
Yellow rope threads heaved on deck in a loose curl
frame his portrait. Under a curlicue crown
he lashed a wind so tight it couldn't scroll away—
he twisted out of every lock.

5.

Pencil tip of the hummingbird is enviable.
Mind its feather, to soar is meaning.
His ruby feeder takes a beating from the rain
while my face toward the starlight
is a rock worn down to the sheen of white bone.
He lifts this sugar through cracked stems.
My own steady drip of clockwork compromises despair.
A bright lure spooled over the rapids
restores a memory I've got to live through.
Like everyone I've brushed against
on dirt paths, in subways, on stairwells, windy
pavement, craggy trail—each a miniscule statistic
who lost so many, each of whom
was cherished, teased, reviled by family or the once beloved.
History, the hidden and distorted,
still cries a bell over Warsaw, or Texas, or the ruins of Aleppo,
icebergs in the tunnels of Manhattan.
I chant a hollow psalm to parchment
before my pen touches: *Unnamed Unacknowledged Hope,*
*let me threadbare and helpless in tendrils*
*coil up moist earth, bind me wrist and ankle*
*to the rock, the tide's rising.*

## 6.

Becalmed all March then breeze wags burst seed,
twigs out of reach, bark twined in deep grooves,
stubble far tipped to the sun
pinches cobalt from the sky.
But the cat in the wind craves bird throat,
'rolls upon prank,' slinks through the kitchen door ajar.
Nodded off in the woodpile,
but stayed alert—as wouldn't we all, if only.

7.

If only I owned a tray full of colors,
all worldly goods aglitter in a tin pail,
but I chose singing for my madness
and leered across a creek-ripped rain field
where hoary pelican scrimmed her masterpiece in the muck
and everywhere flamed toothy aster, horns and debonair
promenades searing my trust, my naïve idiocy.
Deranged by this salt poetry,
I camped here in rain light.

## THE WOMAN WHO HOBBLED IN

A small person with gray hair clipped
since the burning of the extermination camps,
she stepped between me and the *Guernica*
I had for fifty years hoped one day to stand before.
Fifty years—I was old enough to carry a gun and vote
when I first unwrapped it,
framed in a small box to my horror,
but now my eyes focus at the back of her head
where some brown seed or a bit of pitch off pines
or wisp of cypress caught and found purchase.
Earlier someone they beat up on the sidewalk
showed me the ladder cobbled out of staples up
the back of his skull,
dust from cracks in the pavement clung to glass shards.
It was all the right hand could do to hold back the left.
Would she mind,
would she even feel a thumb and index finger
tweeze the bit of crackled matter out of her combed hair?
A piece of her own dream
seeped from the bomb in the eye of the *Guernica* horse
as the man in gunnery school uniform
paraded over a lost crevice at Museo Reina Sofia.
By breakfast she'd grown out of one life
and into another no one foresaw—my kiss like a suitor's
on the fine tan skin of that slender hand
portends I have something magnificent to say,
but utter a word and I'm carried back to her head and it was
all I could do—I had all I could do to keep my hands
out of her hair to keep from stealing that seed.

3.

## A White Confession

I might have looked the part to them,
daydreamer at the top of a gully folded in sunset-
streaked trees, buzzard shadows fanned acres of gravel.
Gesturing toward my house, my dome of wind and light,
*You Captain of this ship?*
joked the larger, more ebullient of the two imposing
not-so-young black men advancing down my driveway
white shirt tails flapping, their ties in loosened Windsor knots.

October dusk alights on the bay, dazzles yachts.
Wind rough as a cat's tongue on an empty can,
a song an idiot howls,
whips through my hair, across their teeth and wary smiles.
The older one divulges how door by door
they've sought our help to pay for college.
*Our* help. *White folks.*
I think I hear the old plantation name,
boot-scraped cheeks on concrete sidewalks under strobe.
The vulture on the upper drafts
without riffle, without shadow.
Bright windows go dull.
*Your neighbor put up two hundred.*

At work I found five dollars.
From my pocket, crumpled on my palm— *I* can *give this.*
In his pale fingers, Lincoln's countenance is not what's needed.
The heftier one who seems so happy wants a *Sprite.*
An innocent, I'd like to be his friend,
but he asks to come inside and see what's in my fridge.
The tiny sky cracks shards of green bottles in paper bags,
a brown sun beneath bent spokes of a bike
peels out on my grass.

No, it's not just race,
not just I refused a drink to the begging man.
But this: late at night under rushing cloud,
swells perforated by stars in such order
we think we see a Great Bear,
their watery eyes weave behind trees—
they could rush me from the shadow.
I bump the door frame,
let a moth spill in before locking four locks and each window.
Along the oak grain stair to the bedroom
(I even recall the Realtor's faux pas: *Master's Bedroom*),
a shining wasp has fallen, stunned by cat,
the species 'White-Faced,'
wasp whose venom bruised my son into shock.
Here, on my filthy glove,
this impossible face, my anaphylactic mirror,
blindly unfolds the story of evil.

## CHILDREN OF THE STORM

They dwell within the acquisition of spirit.
Until it transforms, they no longer need
pen and paper. Or a voice.

They came with cash. She drove.
The man was in love, his world ricocheted
beyond metaphor and jokes.

They bought my desk—loved its surfaces.
They'll polish it, snug in a cabin.
Up here since Katrina, off soon to Montana.

He had a patch on his eye.
Not looking forward to
(his pun) detached retina surgery.

He speaks with a whispered inflection:
*Kind of a Cyclops today.*
His old dog on a rug in the van filled with questions.

Why a desk? I didn't ask. But why Montana?
Ghost write a billionaire cowboy memoir?
And why cart this sarcophagus?

Wish I'd shown some sympathy for the eye.
Or his Homeric allusions. She's loved him at least
the dog's whole life. She hunted this desk, after all.

She and Polyphemus will lug it over twelve steps.
Is that how they met?
Sobered up and blasted out of New Orleans?

It swells their estate of antiques.
A gun rack great-grandfather milled,
a thing he'll never pawn.

Gentle people, small talk.

## AFTER THE TREMORS

We were speaking about the earthquake.
Some were in high school then, others
on a farm, one driving. Few couldn't recall.

A big TV swung on the classroom wall.
A hand rolled above a plate of corn brought back waves
in the tulip fields, yellow and magenta trough and crest.

We have no tornadoes or hurricanes. A blizzard's an insult.
We have floods, we fill sandbags. For earthquakes, drills.
Warned of Tsunami, we alone are ready.

I asked if I might tell my dream and began
though someone groaned: Crusaders' lances on the march,
mountains revolve about the city.

An insect in a helmet raises motorcycle exhaust.
Genied in rich purple, the exhaust oozed to a stately cloud.
A zeppelin contraption spun my way, alone on a dusty path.

Swift across summer air it swam, my cloud in tow.
I turned to run back down the mountain but metal heat
woke me. They laughed: *You awoke before danger killed you.*

*A real dream, nothing happens. Pass the potatoes.*
*Has the vatic songbird at the end of the table finally shut up?*
All through dessert I didn't utter another word.

## TIM AMONG THE MECHANICALS

*My dear Elpenor! My poor, idiotic Elpenor!* —George Seferis

He was my student
run down by a train
he couldn't hear.

I know that engineer's pain.
He howls from a cave,
clutches when he does dream

at controls, keeps a twig fire
near his own inert core,
eyes dull, dull ember.

Called on, the boy
never looked up.
Just waggled his fingers.

Ears cuffed by headgear
though forbidden by our Discipline
kept him safe, he said, or deaf

*to brain spasms of machine-heads,*
but finally, to the engineer's quaver—
or warning or curse—to whistle blast.

Forty years ago, a Chief engineer
in actual peaked stripe cap
and neckerchief, cliché bib overalls,

sang me an aria, and gave me a lift
across the Utah freight yard.
In crushed road-rock,

my pack wobbled
to locomotive quake—
that Chief would have saved him,

would have barked his ears,
that boy, that Tim,
that self-deaf fool.

Lost his life for headphones.
Trespassed on railroad track.

And this is my country.

# Two Rivers

*I felt a kind of dry tenderness of time*—John Fowles

Police car lights at the dip in the road,
three women in sky blue bathrobes, arms folded,
children in pajamas and gloves,
the tall officer's adolescent face,
the horse's halter looped on a girl's wrist,
and the boy in the driveway wrapped in army blanket—
he was the one—he raced dark fields to rescue her stray,
his expression in eerie blue cop-car light
flattened and hard as a weapon.
Our tires crackle over their gravel,
while this morning's detached radio voice
recounts a drowning: someone waist-deep in the Green River
whose boot sole skidded on river-bottom rock.
*Whoa!* accidentally his last word
the moment his mind has speared its crossed heart,
current encircling 'emptied itself neatly into his waders,'
said one witness to its weighing flow.
His legs gave way, his red hat swept past a maple branch
and the river took him.
Strangers reached out with their poles,
watched till his blond head vanished.
He was next to us then gone,
fly rod above the animal a river is
whips unfinished circles as the river insists,
slow spirals brim to the chest, to torn waders.
Slow, familiar as my own nature,
a level unhampered surface consuming a river's brown soul
but no river pours itself out.
I'm gone so it takes me.

*for Frank Moffett, Gerry Demers & George Stanton*

Beneath the first ice, nine clear inches thick,
the river swept a fish below my shoes.
We would lace up tomorrow,
but I never skated that far
where the Miles fed the pond.
That's a little heaven I intended to get back to—
me, the kid filling up with sunlight.
I was a crystal in that pickerel's eye
as she fled below my leather soles.
We skidded away—boys in jackets and ties,
we scuffed up the ice.

# A Prayer for the Republic in Despair

Rats on glue traps in the kitchen beg release.
The house empty except their squeal.
Bolt the cabinets, wait till dawn.
Abandon it, they're in the ceiling, drop from high places.
Not Bubonic rats, not Middle Ages, but Eternal Rat.
No movie rat, not Orwell's torture.
Torturers cut with humiliation.
Not a city dumpster, no sewer, no metaphor.
I brought them in myself—plowing the thicket.
By morning, stealthy frantic swimmers on glue
bite my red leather glove.
One drops on the kitchen floor.
Can no one awaken this death scream?
They get no proper burial—
not allegory, not soldiers in the rain.
War goes away, comes back.
Vermin invasion both ways.
Screams all the way to the garbage.
Rats. These were rats.
Like everybody else, they hated their deaths.

## WATCHING THE OSPREY

The television at the West Szeged apartment
burst with September 11th flames and smoke.
Cacophonous Magyar broadcasters explained
while we could fathom nothing, and next morning
the formal silence throughout Europe
screamed at my despairing language students.
I told how bright throngs of salmon
returned to spawn near my home
and clog a barely flowing stream.
At year's end, invited to the Budapest Writers Union,
I read poems in praise of cluttered eagles' nests
and that genius thistle-webbed thimble
hummingbirds thread to cup a triplet of eggs
while monkey-wrenched log skimmers up on the next parcel
cranked up engines, drenched us in run-off and soil.
I read to polite men and women who,
after centuries of occupation, were kind
to correct a phrase or two of my translations—
Pilinszky Janos hauling the holocaust to an incinerator.
By then, our missiles launched over the head of Sadam
and 'first historical people,' as Hegel proclaimed of Persia.
Primordial human society had erupted
while my suburban passions flared.
Big tree-fallers excavated primeval forests
while tractors rolled off the Pure Land.
Children were marched to the camps,
looped with wire, parents incarcerated,
while three osprey, white whirled-in-grace fish hawks,
chirped—chirped for one another—a warning, directions, or joy
and wheeled above the sunlit clear-cut.

43

## LATE TWENTIETH CENTURY

Lost in Auschwitz-Birkenau one Polish winter
touring the troughs where the women washed,
I panicked, trapped in hut after hut,
but forced myself to walk around those tiers of bunks,
boots grinding the dirt, cold in a parka.

They clung through veils of skin.
Did they ever sleep? Could they dream?
I've never known real fear,
but I was afraid of my ignorance.

Tender wound of history, a torn membrane,
we can't see under the dressing—call it a wing,
and how to navigate this stroll?
A back wing, then, of the hospital
where nothing will grow.

In Vienna, two police in dapper blues
roust a little girl, a gypsy entranced by her violin.
Vivaldi on the street.
Our Schillings clink in her up-ended top hat.

Later, at Heldenplatz where little Hitler made clear
what Europe was in for *(I report to history,*
Fuhrer intoned from Hapsburg's balcony),
we slipped away, and off to Carnival.

Wild Austrians on Ferris Wheels, sanitized displays.
At a booth, my son and I shot arrows
for a stuffed rhinoceros, the attendant encouraging:
*Try again, try again—again.*
We missed the bull's eye, and at last set down our bows.

*One Hundred and Thirty-five Euros, please, Sir.*

But—you said, Try again. —I thought the arrows must be…

*No, Sir. Pay, please.*

But I refused. And he was less than friendly.

Next, he began to beseech: *Please, Sir.*
*The owner video-tapes sales. I'll lose my job.*

But I refused.
Soon we were at, *You will pay me NOW!*

Innocent of this world, my little boy looked to me,
never questioned— *Okay, Teddy, let's run!*
And into the crowded Promenade we disappeared,
we two, we filthy Americans.

## To the Father
### of The Drowned Refugee Child

Years ago, I was in someone's car late at night.
Saddened by the party, we stuck our heads
out both windows and screamed
as we sped along the only street on that island
into the bleak night fields, her bent headlight
skewed toward hawks, mice, clear dripping stars
and we, we were young, innocent, out of touch
with the families who gave us these bodies.
What was so important? Why were we sad?
Moonrise, and we went on screaming.
What in the world mattered so much?

## Born With

A year before he died he called to praise,
rare thing, firemen in the night.
Heavy rubber gear, out of blowing snow
they tromped through his parlor.
Up the crooked oak stair twisted four men,
oxygen barrels strapped, first aid buckets, stretchers,
Gatorade & water jugs, ham & egg sandwiches—
extra frozen gloves, yellow dented flashlights
swung from belts and suspenders.
They came when he called out
(*Nine-One-One* he announced
slow enough I couldn't miss
he hadn't ever called for help,
wouldn't let them in
that time he fell in the kitchen
too weak to clutch the sink,
lay forty-eight hours
in stale beer, pungent urine).

They came through the howler—winter a curse off ocean-
    driven snows,
sea wall crushed on, hour by iced hour, wave on top of wave.
A spray on his porch so nonchalant was ironically gentle.
In strobe light emergency they bustled in,
burley friendly guys, meaty fists lugged soot-pocked helmets,
one of them bandy-legged with a worried smile—and up
he said, right up the steps to the bedroom,
the old marriage bed emptied—
he wouldn't have mentioned to them

much less to me—thirty years ago,
the room itself draped in dust and salt rot,
or that he slept in a room even noisier—
howl of ghost winters gurgled
sea rash, wave toss, rock crack—
a gaggle in the old man's dream—he awakened to
either dead tooth wind or a mambo shark snout crash
caved in his crackling lacework of a window whistling
a befouled round emptiness into his upstairs.

*And they got here,* he went on to praise,
in ten minutes, hailing them as brave young men
out on a night like this, *brave* men, and *kind,* he raved
who almost never thought about the lives of others,
no longer left his house, and in that bedroom *couldn't
believe what they heard*—stallion fury
screech up a window-hole
whipped portraits and cobwebbed heirlooms off the walls,
smashed a mirror—*seven years* more *bad luck.*
The invisible become real in a swarm of winds
wiped out thirty years of spiders,
twirled the arms off retired business suits,
faded paisley ties' once-crisp tongues chattered into snow,
shoes flapped against bureau drawers yanked open,
spilled medallions awarded in seventh grade
(his own hero medals crammed so deep
only death and the devil could disinter).
Spun against the ceiling, a cyclone
of yellowish papers— letters in my self-indulgent hand,
four decades ago from New Jersey.

He called that day to praise their genius:
while the bandy-legged fireman crowed out loud relief—
no blood on the floor, no stroke, no paddles to the heart—
the other one, *a big bruiser* who spoke kindly,
*hoicked up the old queen mattress,*
launched it square inside the empty window dormer,
dug in a bucket where the orange screw gun
                                  hid under First Aid poultices
and fabricated a barricade
                    out of bed boards and plastic tarpaulins
against prolonged assault in blizzard-hurricane,
*at least for now.*

They checked his pulse, strapped him
to the portable blood machine,
shone a beam in his insomniac eye,
gave sandwiches and water bottles and
all four hoisted back onto the strobe-lit firetruck.
*Do they show up like this for anybody?* Just
showed up—out here in misery and weather, for you, Dad
in shatter, your last agonies
                    already begun, firemen in the night
whose report on the call would read
*wedged the bridal-bed inside a window*
against the hundred-year storm—because you needed them,
and spoke kindly to you
when you needed them to
when you called.

## The Virgin Knife

I was always just a cabaret singer off the street
in my loose chemise of tribal songs.
My dog shakes seawater, snout to tail,
and sprays the Muses over you.
Effortless as a silken tent in the breeze,
we'll howl for you this greasy dirge.

I once knew a master
of the art of chanterelle
who dropped a sack of dirt
on my blue-lined foolscap,
forest meat tendered by some roots,
soiled under hunter thumbprint.

You'd never complain of such dinner.
He followed no trail you could forage—
not-so-soaked mud, shade of old growth.
Sunlight slant, fallen orange needles
sprout their cluster's delicate wiggle,
good with fish.

Long after I drop into this valley
*like a high fly ball,*
let the rainbow buses hide behind posts,
city freaks slither under barbwire,
their sandals in muck cowplops
where the psychedelics grow.

But the only true mushroom spy I know,
sworn to secrecy, hunted off-trail.
Pickup in camo and cedar boughs,

he snaked beneath outposts,
slinked past duck hunts.

Kept hidden where chanterelles grow,
his feet up on a workbench,
while a greenhouse lean-to transistor hummed,
*Mariners fry the Red Sox—*

*Can't show you*
*I'd like to, but I won't*
*Find your own*
*Here's a bucketful*
*Don't overdo the butter*

Olive beret, a trek through the high grass
where no one goes, a last look
over the primal shoulder—
*Après moi, le deluge,* he lisped the kingly joke
and, responsible to the world,
he finally wanted to tell, but, incoherent,
fumbled last directions escaped him
and his trove still thrives,
thrives in the sump of aching.

I can hardly keep from dropping a word of praise here—
sharp folds of our ersatz maps crinkle
across steering wheels on his, or any such, hillside pullout.

When I unsheathe my pure blade,
having come so far only to shed everything,
highways burn yet another detour,

plunge wild up the Yukon,
crossroad Devils trade guitar licks
where we scurry down a monk's deer trail
into some deeper Kentucky, lost in the crowd.
Praise those, sans teeth sans eyes,
waltzing past me and the dog on the stage,
sweet imbeciles who burst onto raw untrained road
with or without the gear
we know we better have on board
for the inevitable breakdown.

*for Art Goodtimes & Janet Clark*

## ONE FOR THE ROAD

Story goes he drove New Hampshire
in a hand-torqued SAAB, the old kind,
sewing-machine size engine, and when it fried,
lugged an extra from his back seat,
bolted it in in the big freeze,
snow half up his ankles.

But I knew him back in the day—back when.
When he tried to leave his wife and kids
and pushed off at midnight from his barstool,
his rusted station wagon pointed east
to cross the Rockies.
*Hasta la Vista* and staggered out,
chiseled ice off the door lock,
crammed behind the steering wheel
and drove into a telephone pole.

Years later, in Massachusetts,
I found a free SAAB shell missing its two-stroke heart.
So, out of his North Conway birch forest,
embedded in snow, he wheezed a donor car in place—
*Twangs like a preacher stirring congregants from sleepwalk,*
*dust and mold kicking up back pews, aching for smoke,*
*but she sings like a cherub on full-throttle.*
He smuggled that crapper across the State line
without a headlight, license plate or
much of a way to stop but a rusted handbrake.
Lashed to the back end of his own impeccable road warrior,
he dragged it by the dark of the moon
to my green shell somebody abandoned like a bad check.

In under half an hour he transplanted that beater engine,
left me sockets to tighten
and crawl back across the continent.
And waved so long, yelled it was a hoot.

*I'll send you some money! —maybe a hundred, fifty for sure!*
But I never got to it, and now he's gone,
my once-drunk friend
who never knew he could have sewn
all the tired distances together,
if he only chugged back across the mountains
one more time, back to us.

4.

## THE DAY MERWIN DIED

I was here at the other end of his island
a visitor who knew nothing and I vainly
waited for word a meeting might be possible
so spent last night long after
he must have turned in one last time
washed clean of myself in his poems
and this morning from shadows under the koa
still had no news and at Po'olenalena
passed with him through his dark music
dove into his clear strange ocean
swam among his seagrass-laddered
secrets and didn't divulge them
even to the deepest soul of a wave

### SNOW ON THE CHUCKANUTS

All it takes is their shape far from where I stop
near a puddle
as the speckled backs of three sparrows
foretell the drift of history
for those foothills dusted by snow
out of a bunched burlap cloud pale as swan's wing
to convince me,
flat-footed and dangling two lugs of groceries,
earth isn't flat anymore and,
what with the moon's oval dish stolen,
rain pelt on my lens dizzies
this apparition of white shoulders
setting off to search the heavens.

## SHAGGY MANE

Hot nights when the bars close
silence is a barking dog.
One turquoise convertible rumbles by.
On a wave, it drifts away.
I almost understand what they whisper.

On my dead-end, my headlights
pass the neighbor's bulldozer,
strike tall stalks and moony heads
when I come 'round hungry,
lay a finger on each cap, say its name.

Strands of hair
rescued in pillows and fists,
health is butter in a pan.
Slice them thin—flakes, legs, the bulbs,
a little soil in the crisp sauté.

(Once, my mushrooms poisoned me.
Vomit like no worst hangover.
Death without insurance.)

Stir them with a wooden spoon—
always butter never margarine—
in a gritty succulence, then a last glass aloft—

To health to its best of luck
      To avoiding medical incarceration
      To the gentle distant road
      To this found, worn out, good Swiss Army Knife

       that makes the cut to dig the bulb
To crinoline dawn's escape
To a hair across an hour
To that robust neighbor
       firing up his generator
       eighty and still gutting the woods
To his happy doctors
To his barking hammer

## SONG 49

The wolves are in the street again,
pacing, sniffing the exhaust in the air,
sniffing the flowers and mailboxes.
A pup cries somewhere downtown.
The heels begin to learn new ways to wear thin.
It's hard to know where to sleep, what to eat,
what that was he was going to say going by: *One*,
and so on—no one starving is ever free.

## THE ANSWER

Sometimes people do tell me what to do
and I, my will a phantom limb,
never listen all that closely,
but follow directions they didn't intend.
Tribal consciousness could've
set me to rights early on—born farther north,
my vision frozen like stump to tundra,
my right to choose seep out with breakup thaw.
But no, I'm down here fudging excuses:
I swallowed the advice and stand corrected
in the whirlwind
when what I'm told is *go there, conquer that.*
The fear you think you're done with.
Fear I might be hiding what the world
sees written on my mouth,
pours from my hands, a stain
aging in this bag of feral whispers,
my answer leaking through the permafrost:
melt inside the fear—all our houses
lift on the tip of the same wave.

## LOST IN A RIVER

One night among the fallen limbs
rain spilled over the Little Quil
and my watch slipped from my wrist,
entered detritus, and ticked
its final moment to a polished stone,
swallowed by sunken leaves.
Knees plunged in silt,
my fists scraped a glacial boulder,
the flashlight jerked into alder leaves,
shot across sheets of rain
and the bulb died in the riffles
over two salmon blistered from exhaustion
who prodded one another upstream
past the boat of foam marooned in a log crook
where pear-shape leaves skim the current,
cling to spawned out carcasses.
I have never been here before, in moss silver groves,
my feet billowed by what fury
downwind of salmon stench, our common burden.
So lost, and strangely familiar, this life.

## MIST, SKAGIT VALLEY

The city embedded, I drive in past low houses,
past pawnshops and second-hand tools, sparring gloves,
red plaid work shirts on a hanger, dust on their sleeves
weighing down any gesture.
In the cracked portrait anxiety touches up
the brows' moons of terror in Ali's famous pose.
I'm already dead when I cruise past the café
where I have no business sitting for a mug filled with leaves.
I want this to be my other body, this mist
up the crag face of Mt. Erie, a veil
just out of my reach
          from the flat roof of Lake Eire Grocery
where I jab, my silk trunks puffed by uprush of traffic breeze,
body of a few moments, divinity of the intersection.
But thick snow fog overtakes me,
wedges the carved ridges of the Chuckanuts,
swoops Swinomish Channel.
Colder to the east the Cascades careen off my windshield
and the riverbed contours a float city
whose citizens ache beside their stick fires,
a shot glass to douse winter virus,
and no one appears to notice the KO'd prizefighter of mist,
flat on his back, stands up and rises into cloud.

## GRACE

She bought an island,
and from their reputation with some Vegas plutocrats,
hired the Orcas crew.
A squall in blowing fog,
swaying pilings juggled the dock.
Down the ferry ramp, angled forty degrees,
Lester winched the smaller tractor taut
and kept his seat up on the Cat—
he had no legs.
Long ago a logger's cable snapped
and scythed above his knees.
Guernsey who'd had too many surgeons as a kid,
his skull a shaved lump upon a lump,
jarred the tractor gears and it leapt forward,
winch yanking its rear end out and onto the dock.
Lester inched the Cat down slowly,
careful for the business yet before them,
it being only six a.m.
To guide him down the ramp he looked to Bob,
hair wet with rain, the scar
where he once shot himself a mangled crater.
Near suicides live on in our two-timing archipelago
at rates no higher than newlyweds in Honolulu.
And Geordie helping Guernsey
was by any standard known
the handsomest man on earth
and the most silent.
Only Lester did the talking.
Polite requests, but orders, nonetheless.
*Would you put it back together, Guernsey?*

*Geordie, grab a toolbox?*
Gusts dropped hefty branches.
Though sun flickered too,
and waves writhed up the dock.
They worked without a break
until she brought late lunch,
a millionairess's feast,
and wondered would the crew eat.
Wheelchair strapped to fender useless
over roots and rocky trails,
Lester looked down from the Cat,
a wad of chew behind his lip.
And the wind calmed, rain stopped.
*Well, you know, we do say Grace.*
She was a little slow, I think, to pick this up.
All those bashed brains, and beauty muzzled.
A walking Lester excised from the family portrait.
And they still prayed?
Which, yes, they did.
Hands held 'round and touching the Cat,
bowed heads under a wrecked wedge cloud,
spears of lead stormed the chapel of cedars.

*for Kevin Ames*

## TENACIOUS SNAG

On this raw cliff face, *battered* is hardly the word.
*Achieved* might do
above the blossom of kelp,
its roots' soft grip on mad inward rock.
I feel it in my sagging muscles:
a mystic wrestler's clench around my neck.
Lodged up there some hundred years beyond the sea,
it twists but doesn't crack.

## THE LAST MASTER

The vet's voice soothes us through euthanasia.
That dogged bristled lip already still
as he slides the painless barbiturate
slowly down the catheter's dank tunnel.
We're past the sniff of bush, piss on tree,
black eye rolled back to the master, last wag,
past the killing praise, softly voiced, *Good Boy,*
that soothes an old man's rage and stops my heart.

# THE DEATH OF A SPARROW HAWK

A swarm of goldfinches, a ruined choir,
whooshed their butter-yellow fans.
The kestrel rang through the yard,
sagged the rippled power line
'til her feather tip dashed away from maples.
Three eagles deprived her of purchase,
wing-spins twice hers flapped like shook flannel.
Unfaithful tango partners, they parried her turns
above the neighbor's roan, narrowing gyres—
tore her from the sky, plumb to thorn,
beside the dog's chewed blue neon ball.

## 11:11

Four sticks, they remind me
I will die forty-nine minutes
before the midnight or noon
of a day near the end
of human history and beyond
that hour or minute a world
begins for those who come late
paid the same as workers
longer on the job to finish
what must be finished before
noon or late-shift pay-off
wages the same for all—
a change of heart just in time—
*Home at last but there is*
*no place and we are here.*

## SPADE

Call one one
and you're honest
as an oak,
or the blade
in topsoil.
Lever the handle
not to strain.
This one, *hecho*
*en Mexico, Enero 07,*
mass produced
at lowest cost
to *Truper*, spade boss,
does a good job, and waits
by the fire pit.
The classic form
inters and removes.
Originally,
it was a spoon.

## ABOUT A SPIDER

Hardly a breath, an exhale, but barely,
up off the sea in fog's damp embrace, throbs
the warp and weft her trembling loom has hid.
Yet now, freckled by dew, rippled like ribs
open to heart ache, no reckless wing's pinned,
but she clambers a string I hardly see
and weaves an immeasurable thinness
to so fine a point she's not really there
when I turn back abruptly, make a wish
and step through, as if a mirror, her web
I'll wear for a hat till, chores done, I'll wipe
with a giggle her silk threads off my hair.

## A Courtship

The male whose gold-brown chest almost glows
against our socked-in morning drab
feeds the duller toned female,
her beak the more discerning of the two,
looming, as they perch on a pole, behind him.
His small face turned back and upward to her,
she plucks from his peck
the crumbs he's mauled of the suet
we spoil them with each morning.
This gesture, almost passionate, seems,
or so I anthropomorphize, like a kiss, a first kiss
among the young who try out tongue-touching
in a game out under the stars,
a twist of the neck and lips in giving
what we have in so endless an abundance
and it starts up here, friendly to the self
in hope and care, you, my other, my One,
will give me back when your mouth overflows.

*for Kathy*

## Insomnia, Quiet House

Out of dark empty rooms upstairs you start to scream.
I rush away from my scribbles at the kitchen table—
asleep, you may be writhing in fear, in anguish
for your sisters, or our son, far down the highway.
Your voice pours over some cliff-face drop-off
then returns breath to its smooth riffle.
Halfway up the dark staircase my tears surprise me—
I'm the one who couldn't dream,
who fled too far to hold you against this howling.
How many nights till love can't find me
shaken by failure and grief?

## On the Removal of Trees

A scent of spruce after this cooling rain
floats off the tire-size rounds
a crew of six brought down
while for two days with revved chainsaws
trapezing in cables two hundred feet up
they delivered cords enough
to outlive our neighborhood's fireplace embers
and lowered limb after limb
spire upon plum spire
by cautious pulley to the raucous chipper
the three three-foot wide trees now nude stumpage
so that high sunlight's tangled wave and stealth
shall no longer dapple our windowsills.

## SNOW MOON

All of the moon—all February's blizzard of moonshine
fallen on needles of fir tips and hemlock crowns—
blazes within this one glint of a raindrop
but also floats the smear across the roughed-up face
where a concrete plinth
bears the tonnage of cedar deck
down through a beam's thirty uncounted rings of years
as forgotten as last month's snow,
down to where the butt end of a six by six
crisp milled shadow
cuts the moon in half, cuts its ghosted shine
into two knob islands of moon lit rain.

## AGAINST A SINGULAR BEAUTY

Always that recitative chirp high in the big trees:
the chipmunk fat on chickadee suet—for generations
year upon year the chirp the same—high in the maple,
bark thick as floorboards in a temple,
a hundred-year grapple above bluff fir, fragrant cedar,
this progenitor maple of the cliff face
clinging to an isolate rock
escarped above the sea's vicious roil of swells
and from a distance we call it beauty,
the ticking beauty of North America,
and we don't have to ask who will speak for it:
even a chipmunk upside down on a crippled trunk
makes it plain she was never warning us off some rough nest,
mouths like oozing sores squashed beneath cord wood
or a scatter of maple leaves and twigs under the hood
where my engine's still warm.
Instead she's dancing on a temple spire, daring us
by that incessant *chirrup* high-pitched recognition of insane
hysteria as we branch out from arbor shadows,
daring us to speak for beauty—
to fall and fly and cross space and time
to skim the white-tooth waves
where persecuted whales muscle the windstorm—crazy
we say of such power before we say how beautiful
by which we mean how unpossessable,
we can't own it, and they taunt us too, our little hearts
when we say beauty and betray our innocence
when we say beautiful and mean our own
immortal lack of purpose.

# LOVE UNDER SHADOW

*Time is the echo of an axe*—Philip Larkin

The thin trunk, sparse limbs, of the young fir
shaded downslope of a grand madrona,
arm-like flesh-like branch waved east
over fallaway gully soil
shadowed itself by a twin madrone,
curved boughs sparked by dawn
and, three times taller, the looming cedar
shadows spider crowds, brown squirrel,
quick-shot sparrow whispers.
Boundless chickadee brave the shade
of the even higher regal maple bare of leaves
but about to bud under two woodpeckers
who knocked all winter.
All downhill from hemlock towers
below a wood of mixed deciduous
where when we're lucky eagles skirt the forest,
or a raven triplet
and last night the suspect barred owl.
Today: warmest equinox on record.
Such phrasing deafens us, numb to spectacle.
My first thought—fire, fear our
dry bone of a dead-end will torch
in the fallen away indulgent parade—
all of us gambling along, overshadowed
by our gain and loss.

## In Spades

*Where the buck turns furiously at the hunter*—Walt Whitman

One morning far from here where my dog prowls the wood
more wreckage beat us down: Arctic melt cracked a glacier,
tsunami skinned an island-nation,
police immolated another teenager.
My tennis shoes drenched, grinding circles into the dew,
I hurled a branch against woodlot stumps.
The emptiness of private rage, a bell singing on the high seas,
blame descending on centuries, extinction grown into habit.
A whistle cracked me like a dream
but not a whistle, too shrill—
a yip from the dog in scattered twigs.
A throaty gush of terror.
Reluctantly, I turned to see her fang curse the gravel spew
from the buck whose antlers wobbled and strained his neck,
hooves splayed—eyes bulged at my jawbone.
I writhed on air to steal a whiff of the wild.
In dogtooth crack they rocketed into the woodlot
and, temples throbbing, I slouched away in my wet shoes.

## Cow Field Mist Dusk

My painting will have no surface.
You will enter it by light.
But the sheet of color seems still
the moment refracted sun
twirls cloud mass and the petals,
dapple accidents on crabapples'
wet black trunks. Light enters, richly,
cow-green fields a lake rises to meet.
There's no distance, sundown finches
wash our street in the song for rain.
In these shades there's no tomorrow
but we let it fall on us uncreated.
I have had a canvas but never a brush.

# NOTES:

The son of Poseidon, Polyphemus the Cyclops, cursed Odysseus leading to the deaths of the crew at Scylla & Charybdis which Rachel Carson locates at the mouth of the Strait of Messina. To make amends, Tiresias told Odysseus, perform a rite far inland involving an oar and an altar to Poseidon. Andromeda, the Constellation whose greatest star goes by the Arabic name Alpheratz ("horse's navel" for its place in the Pegasus constellation), was named for the daughter of Cassandra, my favorite mythic figure, condemned to speak truth and never be believed. She's with us still. Lately called Greta. The youngest of Odysseus' mates, Elpenor, distracted, fell from a roof and later turned up in the Land of the Dead. Cobh is the site from which virtually all Irish emigres cast off, as did the Lusitania and Titanic. Maze Goal was the site of the Hunger Strike where IRA prisoners, the poet Bobby Sands among them, died of starvation. Water Street & Taylor is the Mount Baker Block in Port Townsend, Washington. "Bob" is Bob Blair, founder of Empty Bowl. Janos Pilinszky witnessed the horrors of the Holocaust, and his life's work, as Hungary's premier poet of the Twentieth century, grew out of that trauma. The Green River begins at Stampede Pass and joins the Duwamish to empty into Eliot Bay in Seattle, while the Miles, a tributary of the Ipswich River in Massachusetts, flows from its source in Beverly through extensive wetlands before reaching Ipswich, where I learned to ice skate. Cid Corman lived in his parents' home for a time near Annabel Street in Dorchester where I imagined I would always be a child, and where now and then a dream takes me back.

# ABOUT THE AUTHOR

 MICHAEL DALEY, who was born and raised in Dorchester, Massachusetts, entered a religious order as a teenager and upon returning to "the world," was wild in the streets, protesting war and imperialism. He traveled the US on freight trains and by hitchhiking and worked at a series of depressing jobs until joining a tree-planting crew on the Olympic Peninsula and helping to found Empty Bowl Press. He later became a teacher at Mount Vernon High School in Skagit County and is now retired. He and his wife and son spent a Fulbright year in Hungary. He holds a bachelor's degree from the University of Massachusetts and an MFA from the University of Washington. In addition to the Fulbright, he's received awards from Seattle Arts Commission, Washington State Arts Commission, The Institute for the Arts in Boston, Bumbershoot, Fessenden Foundation, National Endowment of the Humanities, Artist Trust, and The Poets House Trust. He lives near Deception Pass in Washington.

*Author photo by Erin Griggs*

For the full Dos Madres Press catalog:
www.dosmadres.com